FIGHT...WIN...SURVIVE

FightWinSurvive.Com

The Prayer Book
(The Power of Prayer)

Steven A. VanDyke

The Bible quotations are from the New King James Version (NKJV) of the Bible.

Disclaimer

This book includes foundational information from various sources and is gathered from education and research. It is published for general reference and is not intended to be a substitute for independent verification by readers when necessary and appropriate.

ISBN-10: 0692205012
ISBN-13: 978-0692205013

Published by:

www.VanDykeEntertainment.com

CONTENTS

ACKNOWLEDGMENTS

In August of 2012 in the middle of the night God gave me a vision for encouraging others. I woke up, turned on my cell phone, typed in what was in my head and went back to sleep. Three words were placed into my mind, and a ministry was birthed into my spirit.

The words Fight…Win…Survive® personally mean more to me than anyone could ever imagine. As a general anxiety sufferer, I often have to rely on those three words for strength, power and daily living. I would like to specially thank my wife Crystal VanDyke, my parents Steven and Carolyn VanDyke, my sister Kimberly VanDyke-Butts and my uncle Sy FitzGerald for their support and patience as I live day to day not knowing what each minute holds in my mind and my body's response to it.

As an encouragement merchandiser and ministry outreach (Fight…Win…Survive®), I hope and pray that each of you who utilizes this book will be empowered to stand fast and stand strong for yourself and for those individuals through prayer for whatever they are facing in this life.

CHAPTER 1
THE POWER OF PRAYER

God speaks to us through His written word, the Bible. We speak to God through prayer. Prayer is one of the most important parts of a Christian's life. Prayer has been defined as "communion with God" and is where we experience a relationship with God.

The purpose of *The Prayer Book* is to provide you with a specific list of individuals who you will pray for by name and situation/circumstance. Everyone has heard the phrase "pray for me" and everyone has made the reply "I will," however when it comes time to pray we often forget who it was that we said we would pray for or what the situation and/or circumstance was that we said we would pray about.

This book allows for 150 prayer entries for you or for individuals who you know and want to petition God on their behalf.

Once you have covered an individual, situation or circumstance in your prayer book, it is suggested that you simply highlight that entry to know that your prayer for that situation, circumstance or individual is no longer needed.

When to Pray

Is anyone among you suffering? Let him pray. Is anyone cheerful? Let him sing psalms. [14] Is anyone among you sick? Let him call for the elders of the church, and let them pray over him, anointing him with oil in the name of the Lord. [15] And the prayer of faith will save the sick, and the Lord will raise him up. And if he has committed sins, he will be forgiven. **James 5:13-15**

How to Pray

"And when you pray, you shall not be like the hypocrites. For they love to pray standing in the synagogues and on the corners of the streets, that they may be seen by men. Assuredly, I say to you, they have their reward. [6] But you, when you pray, go into your room, and when you have shut your door, pray to your Father who is in the secret place; and your Father who sees in secret will reward you openly, [7] And when you pray, do not use vain repetitions as the heathen do. For they think that they will be heard for their many words. [8] "Therefore do not be like them. For your Father knows the things you have need of before you ask Him. [9] In this manner, therefore, pray:

Our Father in heaven,
Hallowed be Your name.
[10] Your kingdom come.
Your will be done
On earth as it is in heaven.
[11] Give us this day our daily bread.

¹² *And forgive us our debts,*
As we forgive our debtors.
¹³ *And do not lead us into temptation,*
But deliver us from the evil one.
For Yours is the kingdom and the power and the glory forever.
Amen.

Praying with the Right Motives

"And whatever you ask in My name, that will I do, that the Father may be glorified in the Son. "If you ask Me anything in My name, I will do it. **John 14:13-14**

You ask and do not receive, because you ask with wrong motives, so that you may spend it on your pleasures. **James 4:3**

CHAPTER 2
THE NINE FORMS OF PRAYER

There are nine forms of prayer that you should be aware of:

1. **Worship**: Seeking God in spirit and in truth.

2. **Confession**: Telling God our sin; specifically telling Him what we did or acknowledging what we failed to have done that should have been done.

3. **Thanksgiving**: Thanking God for what He has done.

4. **Praise**: Declaring the good things about God (His character [who He is] and His actions).

5. **Petition**: Asking for what is desired.

6. **Intercession**: Praying for the needs of others and the advancement of God's interests.

7. **Waiting**: Being and standing still holding steadfast for God to move or speak on something.

8. **Warfare**: The powers of darkness are out to destroy. Command them to be bound or to leave situations and/or circumstances.

9. Praying in Tongues: A method available to those said to be baptized in the Holy Spirit.

CHAPTER 3
THE TWELVE NAMES OF GOD

1. Elohim: "Creator"

The Hebrew word "El" means "mighty," "strong," "prominent." This word "El" itself is translated "God" some 250 times in the Bible and frequently in circumstances which especially indicate the great power of God.

"In the beginning God created the heavens and the earth." Genesis 1:1

2. Adonai: "Master"

The name "Adonai" is translated "Lord" and signifies ownership or mastership. It indicates the truth that God is the owner of each member of the human family, and that He consequently claims the unrestricted obedience of all.

"and said, 'My Lord, if I have now found favor in Your sight, do not pass on by Your servant." Genesis 18:3

3. Jehovah-Jireh: "Provider and My Vision"

In the name, "Jehovah-Jireh," the word "jireh" is simply a transliteration of a Hebrew word which appears many times throughout the Scriptures. Its meaning is simply a form of the verb "to see." As the One who possesses eternal wisdom and knowledge, God knows the end from the beginning. From eternity to eternity he "foresees" everything.

"And Abraham called the name of the place, The-LORD-Will-Provide; as it is said to this day, "In the Mount of the LORD it shall be provided." Genesis 22:14

4. Jehovah: "Father"

The name Jehovah is derived from the Hebrew verb "havah," "to be," or "being." This word is almost exactly like the Hebrew verb, "chavah," (to live), or "life." One can readily see the connection between "being" and "life".

"And the LORD God formed man of the dust of the ground, and breathed into his nostrils the breath of life; and man became a living being." Genesis 2:7

5. Jehovah-M'Kaddesh: "My Sanctifier"

The name "Jehovah-M'Kaddesh" means "Jehovah who sanctifies." The term "sanctify" occurs frequently in the Old Testament. Its primary meaning is "to set apart" or "separate."

"Consecrate yourselves therefore, and be holy, for I am the LORD your God. [8] And you shall keep My statutes, and perform them: I am the LORD who sanctifies you." Leviticus 20: 7-8

6. **El-Shaddai: "My Supply, My Nourishment"**
   Once again, this word "el" is translated by such words as "might" and "power." The word "Shaddai" itself occurs forty-eight times in the Old Testament and is translated "almighty." The Hebrew meaning of the root word in Shaddai ("Shad") is translated "breast." Thus the title "Shaddai" signifies one who "nourishes," "supplies" or "satisfies." Connected with the word for God, "El," then becomes the "One mighty to nourish, satisfy, supply."

   "When Abram was ninety-nine years old, the LORD appeared to Abram and said to him, "I am Almighty God; walk before Me and be blameless." Genesis 17:1

7. **Jehovah-Rohi: "My Shepherd"**
   The name "Jehovah-Rohi" means "Jehovah my Shepherd." It is that most precious designation of Jehovah which begins the twenty-third Psalm, where it is translated, "The Lord is my shepherd." The primary meaning of the word "Ro'eh" is "to feed" or "lead to pasture," as a shepherd does his flock.

"The LORD is my shepherd; I shall not want." Psalms 23:1

8. **Jehovah-Tsidkenu: "My Righteousness"**
   The name "Jehovah-Tsidkenu" means "Jehovah our righteousness." It appears in Jeremiah's prophecy of a "righteous Branch" and a "King" who is to appear. The word "tsidkenu" is derived from "tsedek" - righteousness. It meant originally to be "stiff" or "straight." It signifies God's dealings with men under the ideas of righteousness, justification, and acquittal.

   "Behold, the days are coming," says the LORD, "That I will raise to David a Branch of righteousness; A King shall reign and prosper, And execute judgment and righteousness in the earth. ⁶In His days Judah will be saved, And Israel will dwell safely; Now this is His name by which He will be called: THE LORD OUR RIGHTEOUSNESS." Jeremiah 23:5-6

9. **Jehovah-Rophe: "My Healer"**
   The name "Jehovah-Rophe" means "Jehovah heals." It is the second of the compound names of Jehovah. The word "rophe" appears some sixty or seventy times in the Old Testament, always meaning "to restore," "to heal," "to cure," as a physician, not only in the physical sense but in the moral and spiritual sense also.

"and said, "If you diligently heed the voice of the LORD your God and do what is right in His sight, give ear to His commandments and keep all His statutes, I will put none of the diseases on you which I have brought on the Egyptians. For I am the LORD who heals you." Exodus 15:26

10. Jehovah-Nissi: "My Banner (Victory)"

A banner, in ancient times, was usually a bare pole with a bright shining ornament which "glittered" in the sun. The word "banner" means "to glisten," among other things. It is translated variously "pole," "ensign" or standard. As an ensign or standard, it was a signal to God's people to rally to Him. It stood for His cause, His battle. It was a sign of deliverance, of salvation.

"And Moses built an altar and called its name, The-LORD-Is-My-Banner;" Exodus 17:15

11. Jehovah-Shalom: "My Peace"

The word "Shalom" is one of the most significant in the Old Testament, its various shades of meaning harmonizing with the doctrine of the atonement as the basis of peace with God.

"So Gideon built an altar there to the LORD, and called it The-LORD-Is-Peace. To this day it is still in Ophrah of the Abiezrites." Judges 6:24

12. Jehovah-Shammah: "My Everything"
The meaning of the name "Jehovah-Shammah" is "Jehovah is there."

"All the way around shall be eighteen thousand cubits; and the name of the city from that day shall be: THE LORD IS THERE." Ezekiel 48:35

CHAPTER 4
THE PRAYER JOURNAL

Date _____/_____/_____

I'm praying for (Name) _____

(Situation)_____

_____.

Date _____/_____/_____

I'm praying for (Name) _____

(Situation)_____

_____.

Date _____/_____/_____

I'm praying for (Name) _____

(Situation)_____

_____.

Date _____/ _____/ _____

I'm praying for (Name) _____

(Situation)_____

_____.

Date _____/ _____/ _____

I'm praying for (Name) _____

(Situation)_____

_____.

Date _____/ _____/ _____

I'm praying for (Name) _____

(Situation)_____

_____.

Date _____/_____/_____

I'm praying for (Name) _____

(Situation)_____

_____.

Date _____/_____/_____

I'm praying for (Name) _____

(Situation)_____

_____.

Date _____/_____/_____

I'm praying for (Name) _____

(Situation)_____

_____.

Date _____ / _____ / _____

I'm praying for (Name) _____

(Situation)_____

_____.

Date _____ / _____ / _____

I'm praying for (Name) _____

(Situation)_____

_____.

Date _____ / _____ / _____

I'm praying for (Name) _____

(Situation)_____

_____.

Date _____/_____/_____

I'm praying for (Name) _____

(Situation)_____

_____.

Date _____/_____/_____

I'm praying for (Name) _____

(Situation)_____

_____.

Date _____/_____/_____

I'm praying for (Name) _____

(Situation)_____

_____.

Date _____/_____/_____

I'm praying for (Name) _____

(Situation)_____

_____.

Date _____/_____/_____

I'm praying for (Name) _____

(Situation)_____

_____.

Date _____/_____/_____

I'm praying for (Name) _____

(Situation)_____

_____.

Date _____/ _____/ _____

I'm praying for (Name) _____

(Situation)_____

_____.

Date _____/ _____/ _____

I'm praying for (Name) _____

(Situation)_____

_____.

Date _____/ _____/ _____

I'm praying for (Name) _____

(Situation)_____

_____.

Date _____/_____/_____

I'm praying for (Name) _____

(Situation)_____

_____.

Date _____/_____/_____

I'm praying for (Name) _____

(Situation)_____

_____.

Date _____/_____/_____

I'm praying for (Name) _____

(Situation)_____

_____.

Date _____/_____/_____

I'm praying for (Name) _____

(Situation)_____

_____.

Date _____/_____/_____

I'm praying for (Name) _____

(Situation)_____

_____.

Date _____/_____/_____

I'm praying for (Name) _____

(Situation)_____

_____.

Date _____/ _____/ _____

I'm praying for (Name) _____

(Situation)_____

_____.

Date _____/ _____/ _____

I'm praying for (Name) _____

(Situation)_____

_____.

Date _____/ _____/ _____

I'm praying for (Name) _____

(Situation)_____

_____.

Date _____/ _____/ _____

I'm praying for (Name) _____

(Situation)_____

_____.

Date _____/ _____/ _____

I'm praying for (Name) _____

(Situation)_____

_____.

Date _____/ _____/ _____

I'm praying for (Name) _____

(Situation)_____

_____.

Date _____/_____/_____

I'm praying for (Name) _____

(Situation)_____

_____.

Date _____/_____/_____

I'm praying for (Name) _____

(Situation)_____

_____.

Date _____/_____/_____

I'm praying for (Name) _____

(Situation)_____

_____.

Date _____/_____/_____

I'm praying for (Name) _____

(Situation)_____

_____.

Date _____/_____/_____

I'm praying for (Name) _____

(Situation)_____

_____.

Date _____/_____/_____

I'm praying for (Name) _____

(Situation)_____

_____.

Date _____/_____/_____

I'm praying for (Name) _____

(Situation)_____

_____.

Date _____/_____/_____

I'm praying for (Name) _____

(Situation)_____

_____.

Date _____/_____/_____

I'm praying for (Name) _____

(Situation)_____

_____.

Date _____/_____/_____

I'm praying for (Name) _____

(Situation)_____

_____.

Date _____/_____/_____

I'm praying for (Name) _____

(Situation)_____

_____.

Date _____/_____/_____

I'm praying for (Name) _____

(Situation)_____

_____.

Date _____/_____/_____

I'm praying for (Name) _____

(Situation)_____

_____.

Date _____/_____/_____

I'm praying for (Name) _____

(Situation)_____

_____.

Date _____/_____/_____

I'm praying for (Name) _____

(Situation)_____

_____.

Date _____/ _____/ _____

I'm praying for (Name) _____

(Situation)_____

_____.

Date _____/ _____/ _____

I'm praying for (Name) _____

(Situation)_____

_____.

Date _____/ _____/ _____

I'm praying for (Name) _____

(Situation)_____

_____.

Date _____/_____/_____

I'm praying for (Name) _____

(Situation)_____

_____.

Date _____/_____/_____

I'm praying for (Name) _____

(Situation)_____

_____.

Date _____/_____/_____

I'm praying for (Name) _____

(Situation)_____

_____.

Date _____/_____/_____

I'm praying for (Name) _____

(Situation)_____

_____.

Date _____/_____/_____

I'm praying for (Name) _____

(Situation)_____

_____.

Date _____/_____/_____

I'm praying for (Name) _____

(Situation)_____

_____.

Date _____/_____/_____

I'm praying for (Name) _____

(Situation)_____

_____.

_____

Date _____/_____/_____

I'm praying for (Name) _____

(Situation)_____

_____.

_____

Date _____/_____/_____

I'm praying for (Name) _____

(Situation)_____

_____.

Date _____/_____/_____

I'm praying for (Name) _____

(Situation)_____

_____.

Date _____/_____/_____

I'm praying for (Name) _____

(Situation)_____

_____.

Date _____/_____/_____

I'm praying for (Name) _____

(Situation)_____

_____.

Date _____/_____/_____

I'm praying for (Name) _____

(Situation)_____

_____.

Date _____/_____/_____

I'm praying for (Name) _____

(Situation)_____

_____.

Date _____/_____/_____

I'm praying for (Name) _____

(Situation)_____

_____.

Date _____ / _____ / _____

I'm praying for (Name) _____

(Situation)_____

_____.

Date _____ / _____ / _____

I'm praying for (Name) _____

(Situation)_____

_____.

Date _____ / _____ / _____

I'm praying for (Name) _____

(Situation)_____

_____.

Date _____/_____/_____

I'm praying for (Name) _____

(Situation)_____

_____.

Date _____/_____/_____

I'm praying for (Name) _____

(Situation)_____

_____.

Date _____/_____/_____

I'm praying for (Name) _____

(Situation)_____

_____.

Date _____/_____/_____

I'm praying for (Name) _____

(Situation)_____

_____.

Date _____/_____/_____

I'm praying for (Name) _____

(Situation)_____

_____.

Date _____/_____/_____

I'm praying for (Name) _____

(Situation)_____

_____.

Date _____/_____/_____

I'm praying for (Name) _____

(Situation)_____

_____.

Date _____/_____/_____

I'm praying for (Name) _____

(Situation)_____

_____.

Date _____/_____/_____

I'm praying for (Name) _____

(Situation)_____

_____.

Date _____/_____/_____

I'm praying for (Name) _____

(Situation)_____

_____.

Date _____/_____/_____

I'm praying for (Name) _____

(Situation)_____

_____.

Date _____/_____/_____

I'm praying for (Name) _____

(Situation)_____

_____.

Date _____/_____/_____

I'm praying for (Name) _____

(Situation)_____

_____.

Date _____/_____/_____

I'm praying for (Name) _____

(Situation)_____

_____.

Date _____/_____/_____

I'm praying for (Name) _____

(Situation)_____

_____.

Date _____/_____/_____

I'm praying for (Name) _____

(Situation)_____

_____.

Date _____/_____/_____

I'm praying for (Name) _____

(Situation)_____

_____.

Date _____/_____/_____

I'm praying for (Name) _____

(Situation)_____

_____.

Date _____/_____/_____

I'm praying for (Name) _____

(Situation)_____

_____.

Date _____/_____/_____

I'm praying for (Name) _____

(Situation)_____

_____.

Date _____/_____/_____

I'm praying for (Name) _____

(Situation)_____

_____.

Date _____/_____/_____

I'm praying for (Name) _____

(Situation)_____

_____.

Date _____/_____/_____

I'm praying for (Name) _____

(Situation)_____

_____.

Date _____/_____/_____

I'm praying for (Name) _____

(Situation)_____

_____.

Date _____/_____/_____

I'm praying for (Name) _____

(Situation)_____

_____.

Date _____/_____/_____

I'm praying for (Name) _____

(Situation)_____

_____.

Date _____/_____/_____

I'm praying for (Name) _____

(Situation)_____

_____.

Date _____/_____/_____

I'm praying for (Name) _____

(Situation)_____

_____.

Date _____/_____/_____

I'm praying for (Name) _____

(Situation)_____

_____.

Date _____/_____/_____

I'm praying for (Name) _____

(Situation)_____

_____.

Date _____/_____/_____

I'm praying for (Name) _____

(Situation)_____

_____.

Date _____/_____/_____

I'm praying for (Name) _____

(Situation)_____

_____.

Date _____/_____/_____

I'm praying for (Name) _____

(Situation)_____

_____.

Date _____ / _____ / _____

I'm praying for (Name) _____

(Situation)_____

_____.

Date _____ / _____ / _____

I'm praying for (Name) _____

(Situation)_____

_____.

Date _____ / _____ / _____

I'm praying for (Name) _____

(Situation)_____

_____.

Date _____/_____/_____

I'm praying for (Name) _____

(Situation)_____

_____.

Date _____/_____/_____

I'm praying for (Name) _____

(Situation)_____

_____.

Date _____/_____/_____

I'm praying for (Name) _____

(Situation)_____

_____.

Date ____/____/____

I'm praying for (Name) _____

(Situation)_____

_____.

Date ____/____/____

I'm praying for (Name) _____

(Situation)_____

_____.

Date ____/____/____

I'm praying for (Name) _____

(Situation)_____

_____.

Date _____/_____/_____

I'm praying for (Name) _____

(Situation)_____

_____.

Date _____/_____/_____

I'm praying for (Name) _____

(Situation)_____

_____.

Date _____/_____/_____

I'm praying for (Name) _____

(Situation)_____

_____.

Date _____/_____/_____

I'm praying for (Name) _____

(Situation)_____

_____.

Date _____/_____/_____

I'm praying for (Name) _____

(Situation)_____

_____.

Date _____/_____/_____

I'm praying for (Name) _____

(Situation)_____

_____.

Date _____/_____/_____

I'm praying for (Name) _____

(Situation)_____

_____.

_____

Date _____/_____/_____

I'm praying for (Name) _____

(Situation)_____

_____.

_____

Date _____/_____/_____

I'm praying for (Name) _____

(Situation)_____

_____.

Date _____/_____/_____

I'm praying for (Name) _____

(Situation)_____

_____.

Date _____/_____/_____

I'm praying for (Name) _____

(Situation)_____

_____.

Date _____/_____/_____

I'm praying for (Name) _____

(Situation)_____

_____.

Date _____/_____/_____

I'm praying for (Name) _____

(Situation)_____

_____.

Date _____/_____/_____

I'm praying for (Name) _____

(Situation)_____

_____.

Date _____/_____/_____

I'm praying for (Name) _____

(Situation)_____

_____.

Date _____/_____/_____

I'm praying for (Name) _____

(Situation)_____

_____.

Date _____/_____/_____

I'm praying for (Name) _____

(Situation)_____

_____.

Date _____/_____/_____

I'm praying for (Name) _____

(Situation)_____

_____.

Date _____/_____/_____

I'm praying for (Name) _____

(Situation)_____

_____.

Date _____/_____/_____

I'm praying for (Name) _____

(Situation)_____

_____.

Date _____/_____/_____

I'm praying for (Name) _____

(Situation)_____

_____.

Date _____/_____/_____

I'm praying for (Name) _____

(Situation)_____

_____.

Date _____/_____/_____

I'm praying for (Name) _____

(Situation)_____

_____.

Date _____/_____/_____

I'm praying for (Name) _____

(Situation)_____

_____.

Date _____/_____/_____

I'm praying for (Name) _____

(Situation)_____

_____.

Date _____/_____/_____

I'm praying for (Name) _____

(Situation)_____

_____.

Date _____/_____/_____

I'm praying for (Name) _____

(Situation)_____

_____.

Date ____/____/____

I'm praying for (Name) _____

(Situation)_____

_____.

Date ____/____/____

I'm praying for (Name) _____

(Situation)_____

_____.

Date ____/____/____

I'm praying for (Name) _____

(Situation)_____

_____.

Date _____/_____/_____

I'm praying for (Name) _____

(Situation)_____

_____.

Date _____/_____/_____

I'm praying for (Name) _____

(Situation)_____

_____.

Date _____/_____/_____

I'm praying for (Name) _____

(Situation)_____

_____.

Date _____/ _____/ _____

I'm praying for (Name) _____

(Situation)_____

_____.

Date _____/ _____/ _____

I'm praying for (Name) _____

(Situation)_____

_____.

Date _____/ _____/ _____

I'm praying for (Name) _____

(Situation)_____

_____.

Date _____/_____/_____

I'm praying for (Name) _____

(Situation)_____

_____.

Date _____/_____/_____

I'm praying for (Name) _____

(Situation)_____

_____.

Date _____/_____/_____

I'm praying for (Name) _____

(Situation)_____

_____.

CHAPTER 5
BIBLE VERSES ON PRAYER

1 Thessalonians 5:17 PRAY WITHOUT CEASING,

Romans 15:30 *Now I beg you, brethren, through the Lord Jesus Christ, and through the love of the Spirit, that you strive together with me in prayers to God for me,*

2 Corinthians 1:11 *you also helping together in prayer for us, that thanks may be given by many persons on our behalf for the gift granted to us through many.*

1 Timothy 2:1-2 *Therefore I exhort first of all that supplications, prayers, intercessions, and giving of thanks be made for all men, [2] for kings and all who are in authority, that we may lead a quiet and peaceable life in all godliness and reverence.*

James 5:13-14 *Is anyone among you suffering? Let him pray. Is anyone cheerful? Let him sing psalms. [14] Is anyone among you sick? Let him call for the elders of the church, and let them pray over him, anointing him with oil in the name of the Lord.*

James 5:16 *Confess your trespasses to one another, and pray for one another, that you may be healed. The effective, fervent prayer of a righteous man avails much.*

Ephesians 6:18 *praying always with all prayer and supplication in the Spirit, being watchful to this end with all perseverance and supplication for all the saints—*

1 Corinthians 14:15 *What is the conclusion then? I will pray with the spirit, and I will also pray with the understanding. I will sing with the spirit, and I will also sing with the understanding.*

James 1:6 *But let him ask in faith, with no doubting, for he who doubts is like a wave of the sea driven and tossed by the wind.*

ADDITIONAL RESOURCES AND RELEASES

*Get *"The Power of Prayer"* by VanDyke Entertainment available on iTunes, Amazon MP3, Google Play and other online retailers.

*Join our prayer group on FaceBook. Search: The Power of Prayer & The Joy of Praise.

*Look for *"Words of Wisdom, Points of Power and Biblical Empowerment"* available on Amazon.com or FightWinSurvive.com.

*Look for *"My Thanksgiving Journal (Thanking God One Day At A Time)"* available on Amazon.com or FightWinSurvive.com.

www.ingramcontent.com/pod-product-compliance
Lightning Source LLC
LaVergne TN
LVHW041326080426
835513LV00008B/607